THIS BIRTHDAY BOOK BELONGS TO...

_____

ADDRESS

_____

_____

_____

_____

TELEPHONE

_____

MOBILE PHONE

_____

EMAIL

_____

BLOOMSBURY CHILDREN'S BOOKS

First publishing in Great Britain in 2001
Bloomsbury Publishing Plc, 38 Soho Square, London, W1D 3HB

ISBN 0 7475 5520 6

Designed by Traffika Publishing Ltd.
Printed by C & C offset

BIRTHDAY
BOOK

JANUARY

1

Jack Bennett

1919 – J. D. SALINGER – Author of **The Catcher in the Rye**

2

1969 – CHRISTY TURLINGTON – American supermodel

3

1892 – J. R. R. TOLKEIN – Author of **Lord of the Rings** and **The Hobbit**

4

1809 – LOUIS BRAILLE – Creator of Braille

5

1938 – KING JUAN CARLOS I OF SPAIN

6

1955 – ROWAN ATKINSON – British actor

7

1964 – NICHOLAS CAGE – American actor

JANUARY

8

1935 – ELVIS PRESLEY – American singer known as "The king of rock'n'roll"

9

1913 – RICHARD NIXON – 37th American president

10

1949 – GEORGE FOREMAN – Oldest heavyweight boxing champion in history

11

1952 – BEN CRENSHAW – Golfer, holder of the most individual amateur golf titles

JANUARY

12

1876 – JACK LONDON – Author of Call of the Wild

13

1926 – MICHAEL BOND – Creator of Paddington Bear

14

1886 – HUGH LOFTING – Creator of Dr Dolittle

15

1929 – MARTIN LUTHER KING – American civil rights activist and Nobel recipient

16

1974 – KATE MOSS – British supermodel

17

1942 – MUHAMMAD ALI – American world heavyweight boxing champion, three times winner

18

1882 – A. A. MILNE – Creator of Winnie the Pooh

JANUARY

JANUARY

19 *grandad Chn .*

1839 – PAUL CEZANNE – French artist

20

1930 – DR EDWIN BUZZ ALDRIN – Second man to walk on the moon

21

1855 – JOHN MOSES BROWNING – Inventor of the Browning automatic pistol

---

22 *Daddy .*

1960 – MICHAEL HUTCHENCE – Lead singer – INXS

23

1832 – EDOUARD MANET – French artist, forerunner of the Impressionist movement

---

24

1712 – FREDERICK II OF PRUSSIA

25

1759 – ROBERT BURNS – Scotland's national poet

JANUARY

26

1925 – PAUL NEWMAN – Actor, racer and popcorn maker!

27

1832 – LEWIS CARROLL – Poet

28

1841 – HENRY STANLEY – British explorer

29

1954 – OPRAH WINFREY – Actress and chat show hostess

30

1937 – BORIS SPASSKY – Former world chess champion

31

1971 – MINNIE DRIVER – British actress

FEBRUARY

1
1915 – STANLEY MATTHEWS – British footballer

2
1650 – NELL GWYNN – Actress, comedienne

3
1821 – ELIZABETH BLACKWELL – First female English doctor

4
1902 – CHARLES LINDBERGH – Made the first transatlantic flight

FEBRUARY

5
1893 – CAPTAIN W. E. JOHNS – World War I pilot and creator of Biggles

6
1945 – BOB MARLEY – Reggae musician

7
1812 – CHARLES DICKENS – English novelist

8
1931 – JAMES DEAN – American actor

9
1909 – CARMEN MIRANDA – Brazilian singer

10
1955 – GREG NORMAN – Australian golfer

11
1969 – JENNIFER ANISTON – American actress, star of Friends

FEBRUARY

12
1938 – JUDY BLUME – American author

13
1974 – ROBBIE WILLIAMS – English pop singer

14
Andy Tibbert

1473 – NICOLAS COPERNICUS – Polish astronomer, discovered the
earth revolves around the sun

15
1954 – MATT GROENING – Creator of the Simpsons

16
1959 – JOHN McENROE – American tennis player

17
1963 – MICHAEL JORDAN – American basketball player

18
1954 – JOHN TRAVOLTA – American actor and dancer

FEBRUARY

19
1960 – PRINCE ANDREW

20
1966 – CINDY CRAWFORD – American supermodel

21
1946 – ALAN RICKMAN – British actor

22
1975 – DREW BARRYMORE – American actress

23
1685 – GEORGE FREDERIC HANDEL – German-born English composer

24
1786 – WILHELM GRIMM – Author of Grimm's Fairy Tales

25
1841 – PIERRE AUGUSTE RENOIR – French painter and sculptor

FEBRUARY

26

1802 – VICTOR HUGO – French Writer

27

1980 – CHELSEA CLINTON – Daughter of Bill Clinton, 42nd president of America

28

1683 – RENE ANTOINE DE REAUMUR – Inventor of the thermometer

29

1840 – JOHN PHILIP HOLLAND – Irish inventor who designed the first submarines for both the US Navy and Royal Navy

FEBRUARY

MARCH

1

1810 – FREDERIC CHOPIN – Polish composer

2

1904 – DR SEUSS – American author of **The Cat in the Hat**

3

1847 – ALEXANDER GRAHAM BELL – Inventor of the telephone

4

1937 – VALENTINA TERESHROVA – First woman in space

5

1133 – HENRY II – King of England (1154 - 1189)

6

1475 – MICHELANGELO BUONAROTTI – Italian sculptor and painter of the Sistine Chapel

7

1872 – PIET MONDRIAN – Dutch artist

MARCH

8

1859 – KENNETH GRAHAME – Author of Wind in the Willows

9

1934 – YURI GAGARIN – Russian – first man in space

10

1958 – SHARON STONE – American actress

11

1885 – SIR MALCOLM CAMPBELL – First motorist to exceed 300 mph

12

1946 – LIZA MINNELLI – American singer and actress

13

1855 – PERCIVAL LOWELL – Astronomer, predicted that there were other planets

14

1879 – ALBERT EINSTEIN – One of the greatest physicists of all time

MARCH

MARCH

15
1767 – ANDREW JACKSON – 7th American president

16
1751 – JAMES MADISON – 4th American president

17
1938 – RUDOLF NUREYEV – Russian ballet dancer

18
1952 – PAT EDDERY – British champion jockey

19
1813 – DAVID LIVINGSTONE – Missionary and explorer

20
1958 – HOLLY HUNTER – American actress

21
1960 – AYRTON SENNA – Brazilian formula one driver

MARCH

22
1948 – SIR ANDREW LLOYD-WEBBER – British composer

23
1929 – SIR ROGER BANNISTER – First man to run a mile in less than 4 minutes

24
1930 – STEVE McQUEEN – American actor

25
1947 – ELTON JOHN – British pop singer

26
1931 – LEONARD NIMOY – American actor – Dr Spock from **Star Trek**

27
1922 – DICK KING-SMITH – British children's author

28
1921 – DIRK BOGARDE – American actor

MARCH

29

1943 – JOHN MAJOR – Former Prime Minister of England

30

1950 – ROBBIE COLTRANE – British actor

31

1971 – EWAN MACGREGOR – British actor

APRIL

1

1932 – DEBBIE REYNOLDS – American actress and singer

2

1960 – LINFORD CHRISTIE – British Sprinter and Olympic medallist

3

1367 – HENRY IV – King of England (1399 - 1413)

4

1821 – LINUS YALE – Inventor of the Yale lock

5

1827 – JOSEPH LISTER – British scientist. First person to use antiseptic to treat wounds

6

1929 – ANDRE PREVIN – Pianist and composer

7

1770 – WILLIAM WORDSWORTH – British poet

APRIL

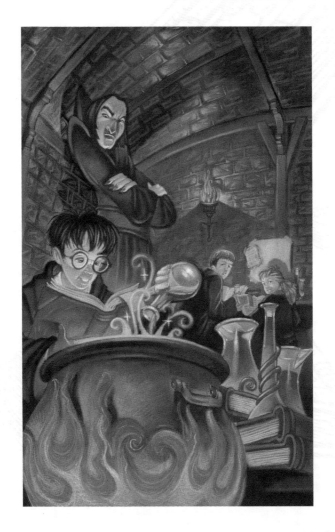

APRIL

8

1912 – SONJA HENIE – Norwegian champion ice skater

9

1971 – JACQUES VILLENUEVE – Canadian formula
one driver

10

1847 – JOSEPH PULITZER – Creator of prize for literature
and journalism

11

1770 – GEORGE CANNING – British Prime Minister who died
after a few months in office

12

1941 – BOBBY MOORE – British footballer

13

1963 – GARRY KASPAROV – Azerbaijani world champion chess player

14

1977 – SARAH MICHELLE GELLER – American actress, star of
Buffy the Vampire Slayer

15

1929 – SIR JOEL CADBURY – Chocolate manufacturer

16

1889 – CHARLIE CHAPLIN – Star of silent movies

APRIL

17

1622 – HENRY VAUGHAN – Welsh poet

18

1976 – MELISSA JOAN HART – American acress - star of Sabrina, the Teenage Witch

19

1935 – DUDLEY MOORE – British actor

20

1893 – JOAN MIRO – Spanish painter

21

Susie Bennett

1926 – ELIZABETH II – Queen of England

22

1916 – YEHUDI MENUHIN – Violinist

23

1564 – WILLIAM SHAKESPEARE – English playwright

APRIL

24
1942 – BARBARA STREISAND – American actress and singer

25
1940 – AL PACINO – American actor

26
1877 – SIR ALLIOT VERDON-ROE – Builder of the first successful British powered aeroplane

27
1791 – SAMUEL MORSE – Inventor of Morse code

28
1442 –EDWARD IV – King of England (1471 - 1483)

29
1970 – ANDRE AGASSI – American tennis player

30
1662 – MARY II – Queen of England (1689 - 1694)

MAY

1

1852 – CALAMITY JANE – American adventuress (Martha J. Burke)

2

1969 – BRIAN LARA – West Indian cricketer

3

1896 – DODIE SMITH– English author of 101 Dalmatians

4

1929 – AUDREY HEPBURN – American actress and ambassador of good will

5

1943 – MICHAEL PALIN – British actor

6

1953 – TONY BLAIR – British Prime Minister

7

1909 – EDWIN HERBERT LAND – American inventor of the Polaroid camera

MAY

8

1884 – HARRY S TRUMAN – 33rd American president

9

1860 – SIR JAMES BARRIE – Scottish writer and author of **Peter Pan**

10

1960 – BONO – Irish pop singer

11

1904 – SALVADOR DALI – Spanish surrealist painter

12

1820 – FLORENCE NIGHTINGALE – established nursing
as a profession

13

1907 – DAPHNE DU MAURIER – Cornish author

14

1944 – GEORGE LUCAS – Writer and director of **Star Wars**

MAY

MAY

15
1856 – LYMAN FRANK BAUM – American creator of The Wizard of Oz

16
1831 – DAVID HUGHES – American inventor of the microphone

17
1961 – ENYA – Singer songwriter

18
1920 – POPE JOHN PAUL II – The first Polish Pope

MAY

19

1963 – YASMIN LE BON – English model

20

1946 – CHER – American actress and singer

21

1904 – FATS WALLER – American jazz musician

22

1859 – SIR ARTHUR CONAN DOYLE – Creator of Sherlock Holmes

23

1966 – GRAEME HICK – English cricketer

24

1819 – QUEEN VICTORIA – Queen of England (1837 - 1901)

25

1889 – IGOR SIKORSKY – Designed the first functional helicopter

MAY

26
1907 – JOHN WAYNE – American actor – renowned for his roles in Westerns

27
1970 – JOSEPH FIENNES – British actor

28
1908 – IAN FLEMING – Creator of James Bond

29
Roy Drew

1917 – JOHN F KENNEDY – 35th American president

30
1908 – MEL BLANC – Voice of animated characters Daffy Duck, Bugs Bunny and others

31
1930 – CLINT EASTWOOD – American actor

JUNE

1

1926 – MARILYN MONROE – American actress

2

1857 – EDWARD ELGAR – English composer

3

1877 – RAOUL DUFY – French painter

4

1738 – GEORGE III – King of England (1760 - 1820)

5

1898 – FEDERICO GARCIA LORCA – Spanish poet and dramatist

6

1935 – THE DALAI LAMA – Spiritual leader of Tibet

7

Cathy Richardson

1940 – TOM JONES – Welsh pop singer

JUNE

8

1869 – FRANK LLOYD WRIGHT – American architect

9

1963 – JOHNNY DEPP – American actor

10

1928 – MAURICE SENDAK – American children's author and illustrator of *Where the Wild Things Are*

11

David Richardson

1910 – JACQUES COUSTEAU – Inventor of the aqualung

JUNE

JUNE

12
1929 – ANNE FRANK – Jewish author

13
1958 – PETER SCUDAMORE – British champion jockey

14
1961 – BOY GEORGE – English pop singer

15
1964 – COURTENEY COX ARQUETTE – American actress, star of Friends

16
1890 – STAN LAUREL – British comedian of silent films

17
1980 – VENUS WILLIAMS – American tennis player

18
1942 – PAUL McCARTNEY – Singer songwriter and ex Beatle

JUNE

19 Isabelle Richardson ~

1947 – SALMAN RUSHDIE – Writer and Booker Prize winner

20

1949 – LIONEL RICHIE – Pop singer songwriter

21

1982 – PRINCE WILLIAM

22

1949 – MERYL STREEP – American actress

23

1894 – EDWARD, DUKE OF WINDSOR – King who abdicated (1936)

24

1895 – JACK DEMPSEY – World heavyweight boxing champion

25

1903 – GEORGE ORWELL – British author of Animal Farm

JUNE

26

1902 – WILLIAM LEAR – American inventor of the car radio

27

1880 – HELEN KELLER – Champion for the blind

28

1491 – HENRY VIII – King of England (1509 - 1547)

29

1900 – ANTOINE DE SAINT EXUPERY – Aviator and author of *The Little Prince*

30

1966 – MIKE TYSON – World champion boxer

JULY

1
1961 – PRINCESS DIANA

2
1489 – THOMAS CRANMER – Archbishop of Canterbury
under Henry VIII

3
1937 – TOM STOPPARD – British playwright

4
1872 – CALVIN COOLIDGE – 30th American president

5
1810 – P. T. BARNUM – American impresario, circus owner

6
1946 – SYLVESTER STALLONE – American actor

7
1940 – RINGO STARR – British musician

JULY

8 Grandma

1951 – ANGELICA HUSTON – American actress

9

1937 – DAVID HOCKNEY – English painter

10

1954 – NEIL TENNANT – British pop singer from The Pet Shop Boys

11

1274 – ROBERT THE BRUCE – Scottish king

12

1937 – BILL COSBY – American comedian

13

1944 – ERNO RUBIK – Creator of the Rubik's cube

14

1858 – EMMELINE PANKHURST – Suffragette

JULY

15

1606 – REMBRANDT VAN RIJN – Dutch artist

16

1872 – ROALD AMUNDSEN – Norwegian explorer –
first person to reach the South Pole

JULY

17

1952 – DAVID HASSELHOFF – American actor, star of Bay Watch

18

1918 – NELSON MANDELA – South African President

19

1834 – EDGAR DEGAS – French painter

20

1919 – SIR EDMUND HILLARY – Explorer, one of first people to ascend Everest

21

1952 – ROBIN WILLIAMS – American comedian and actor

22

1947 – DANNY GLOVER – American actor

JULY

23
1892 – HAILE SELASSIE – Ethiopian emperor

24
1897 – AMELIA EARHART – first woman to cross the Atlantic in an aeroplane

25
1967 – MATT LEBLANC – American actor, star of **Friends**

26
1943 – MICK JAGGER – Singer songwriter and Rolling Stone

27
1824 – ALEXANDRE DUMAS – French novelist – writer of **The Three Musketeers**

28
1866 – BEATRIX POTTER – British children's author

29
1841 – ARMAUER GERHARD HENRIK HANSEN – discoverer of the bacillus causing leprosy

JULY

30

1863 – HENRY FORD – American motorcar manufacturer

31

1965 – J. K. ROWLING – British children's author

AUGUST

1
10BC – CLAUDIUS I – Roman emperor

2
1820 – JOHN TYNDALL – British scientist who discovered why the sky is blue

3
1811 – ELISHA GRAVES OTIS – American inventor of the lift

4
1900 – QUEEN ELIZABETH THE QUEEN MOTHER

5
1930 – NEIL ARMSTRONG – First man to walk on the moon

6
1928 – ANDY WARHOL – American pop art artist

7
Grandma Mary

1876 – MATA HARI – Dutch dancer and spy

AUGUST

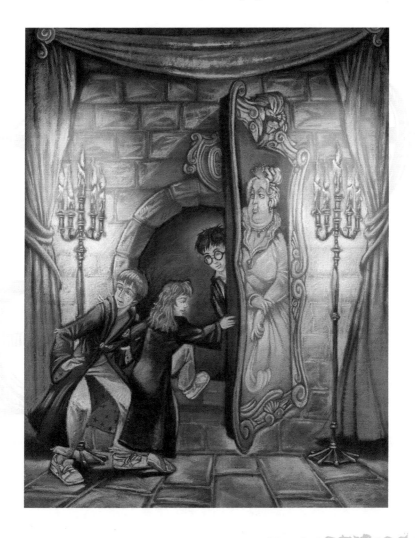

AUGUST

SCABBERS™

8

1953 – NIGEL MANSELL – British formula one racer

9

1963 – WHITNEY HOUSTON – American pop singer

10 Mum

1960 – ANTONIO BANDERAS – Spanish actor

AUGUST

11
1897 – ENID BLYTON – Children's author

12
1971 – PETE SAMPRAS – Tennis player

13
1970 – ALAN SHEARER – British footballer

14
1950 – GARY LARSON – Cartoonist of the Far Side

15
1769 – NAPOLEON BONAPARTE – French president

16
1958 – MADONNA – American pop star

17
1786 – DAVY CROCKETT – American frontiersman and politician

AUGUST

18

1774 – MERIWETHER LEWIS – American explorer of a route to the Pacific Ocean

19

1969 – MATTHEW PERRY – American actor, star of Friends

20

1833 – BENJAMIN HARRISON – 23rd American president

21

1872 – AUBREY BEARDSLEY – British illustrator

22

1934 – NORMAN SCHWARZKOPF – American army general

23

1754 – LOUIS XVI – King of France

24

1929 – YASSER ARAFAT – Palestinian leader

AUGUST

25

1930 – SEAN CONNERY – Scottish actor

26

1980 – MACAULAY CULKIN – American actor, star of **Home Alone**

27

1910 – MOTHER TERESA – Tireless worker for the homeless and destitute

28

1958 – LENNY HENRY – British comedian and actor

29

1958 – MICHAEL JACKSON – American singer songwriter

30

1797 – MARY SHELLEY – English author of **Frankenstein**

31

1870 – MARIA MONTESSORI – Italian educator and pioneer in children's education

SEPTEMBER

1

1923 – ROCKY MARCIANO – American boxer, only undefeated heavyweight champion

2

grandud Tibbesr

1965 – LENNOX LEWIS – Boxing champion

3

1875 – FERDINAND PORSCHE – Car designer

4

1895 – NIGEL BRUCE – British Actor, Dr Watson in Sherlock Holmes

5

1847 – JESSE JAMES – American outlaw

6

1766 – JOHN DALTON – English chemist who put forward the atomic theory

7

1533 – ELIZABETH I – Queen of England (1558 - 1603)

SEPTEMBER

SEPTEMBER

8

1925 – PETER SELLERS – British actor, star of The Pink Panther

9

1960 – HUGH GRANT – British actor

10

1753 – SIR JOHN SOANE – Architect of Bank of England

11

1885 – D. H. LAWRENCE – British author

12

1818 – RICHARD GATLING – Inventor of first machine gun

13

1916 – ROALD DAHL – British author

14

1947 – SAM NEILL – Irish born New Zealand actor

15
1890 – AGATHA CHRISTIE – British crime writer

16
1956 – DAVID COPPERFIELD – American illusionist

SEPTEMBER

17

1960 – DAMON HILL – Former British champion racing driver

18

1905 – GRETA GARBO – Swedish actress of early Hollywood films

19

1911 – WILLIAM GOLDING – Author of **Lord of the Flies**

20

1934 – SOPHIA LOREN – Academy Award winning actress

21

1947 – STEPHEN KING – American author

22

1515 – ANNE OF CLEVES – The fourth wife of Henry VIII

23

1949 – BRUCE SPRINGSTEEN – American singer songwriter

SEPTEMBER

24
1936 – JIM HENSON – Creator of the Muppets

25
1943 – MICHAEL DOUGLAS – American actor

26
1887 – SIR BARNERS WALLIS – British inventor of the bouncing bomb

27
1947 – MEAT LOAF (Marvin Aday) – American singer

28
1934 – BRIGITTE BARDOT – French actress

29
1956 – SEBASTIAN COE – Former British Olympic athlete, member of parliament

30
1852 – SIR CHARLES VILLIERS STANFORD – Irish composer

OCTOBER

1

1935 – JULIE ANDREWS – Singer, actress, activist for children's rights

2

1869 – MAHATMA GANDHI – Indian political activist

3

1973 – NEVE CAMPBELL – American actress

4

1946 – SUSAN SARANDON – American actress

5

1954 – BOB GELDOF – Irish singer and International famine relief organiser

6

1973 – IOAN GRUFFUDD – Welsh actor

7

1931 – DESMOND TUTU – South African religious leader

OCTOBER

8

1943 – R. L. STINE – American author

9

1940 – JOHN LENNON – Beatle, singer songwriter

10

1970 – MATTHEW PINSENT – British rower and three times Olympic gold medallist

OCTOBER

OCTOBER

11
1937 – Sir BOBBY CHARLTON – British footballer

12
1935 – LUCIANO PAVAROTTI – Operatic singer

13
1925 – MARGARET THATCHER – Former British Prime Minister

14
1633 – JAMES II – King of England (1685 - 1689)

15
1881 – P. G. WODEHOUSE – British comic writer

16
1854 – OSCAR WILDE – Irish writer

17
1915 – ARTHUR MILLER – American playwright, husband of Marilyn Monroe

OCTOBER

18
1956 – MARTINA NAVRATILOVA – Tennis champion

19
1946 – PHILIP PULLMAN – Children's author

20
My birthday

1632 – SIR CHRISTOPHER WREN – Architect of St Paul's Cathedral

21
1833 – ALFRED NOBEL – Inventor, with his father, of torpedoes and mines, then the Nobel Peace Prize

22
1811 – FRANZ LISZT – Hungarian composer and pianist

23
1940 – PELE – Brazilian footballer

24
1936 – BILL WYMAN – Rock star, member of the Rolling Stones

OCTOBER

25
1881 – PABLO PICASSO – Spanish artist

26
1947 – HILLARY CLINTON – US senator and wife of 42nd US president

27
1728 – JAMES COOK – British explorer

28
1955 – BILL GATES – Owner of Microsoft computer company

29
1971 – WINONA RYDER – American actress

30
1960 – DIEGO MARADONA – Argentinian footballer

31
1930 – MICHAEL COLLINS – American astronaut who commanded the first moon landing

NOVEMBER

1 1762 – SPENCER PERCEVAL – The only British Prime Minister to have been assassinated

2 1755 – MARIE ANTOINETTE – Queen of France

3 1718 – EARL OF SANDWICH – Gave his name to the sandwich

4 1969 – MATTHEW McCONAUGHEY – American actor

5 1935 – LESTER PIGGOTT – British champion jockey

6 1861 – JAMES NAISMITH – Inventor of basketball

7 1867 – MARIE CURIE – Scientist, researcher, Nobel Prize winner

NOVEMBER

NOVEMBER

8

1656 – EDMUND HALLEY – English astronomer who gave his name to the comet

9

1841 – EDWARD II – King of England (1901 - 1910)

NOVEMBER

10
1942 – TIM RICE – British Composer

11
1974 – LEONARDO DICAPRIO – American actor

12
1966 – DAVID SCHWIMMER – American actor, star of Friends

13
1850 – ROBERT LOUIS STEVENSON – Scottish novelist and poet

14
1948 – PRINCE CHARLES

15
1890 – RICHMAL COMPTON – Author of the Just William stories

16
1961 – FRANK BRUNO – British boxer

NOVEMBER

17

1944 – DANNY DE VITO – American actor

18

1835 – SIR WILLIAM GILBERT – One half of famous opera
writers Gilbert and Sullivan

19

1942 – CALVIN KLEIN – Clothing designer

20

1842 – SIR JAMES DEWAR – Scottish inventor of the vacuum flask

21

1945 – GOLDIE HAWN – American actress

22

1890 – CHARLES DE GAULLE – French president

23

Twins B'day

1859 – BILLY THE KID – American outlaw

NOVEMBER

24
1849 – FRANCES HODGSON BURNETT – Author of The Secret Garden

25
1914 – JO DIMAGGIO – American baseball hero, second husband of Marilyn Monroe

26
1922 – CHARLES SCHULZ – Creator of Snoopy

27
1942 – JIMI HENDRIX – American rock star

28
1959 – JUDD NELSON – American actor

29
1832 – LOUISA MAY ALCOTT – Author of Little Women

30
1874 – WINSTON CHURCHILL – Former British Prime Minister

DECEMBER

1
1935 – WOODY ALLEN – American actor

2
1981 – BRITNEY SPEARS – Canadian pop singer

3
1753 – SAMUEL CROMPTON – English inventor of the cotton-spinning machine

4
1949 – JEFF BRIDGES – American actor

5
1901 – WALT DISNEY – Creator of the cartoon company

6
1958 – NICK PARK – Creator of Wallace and Gromit

7
1598 – GIAN LORENZO BERNINI – Italian Baroque sculptor

DECEMBER

8

1966 – SINEAD O'CONNOR – Irish pop singer

9

1934 – DAME JUDI DENCH – British actress

10

1960 – KENNETH BRANAGH – English actor

11

1757 – CHARLES WESLEY – English composer and organist

12

1915 – FRANK SINATRA – American singer and dancer

13

1925 – DICK VAN DYKE – American actor and dancer, star of **Mary Poppins**

14

Uncle Steve

1979 – MICHAEL OWEN – British footballer

DECEMBER

DECEMBER

15
1970 – FRANKIE DETTORI – Italian born champion jockey

16
1775 – JANE AUSTEN – British author

17
1945 – JACQUELINE WILSON – Children's author

18
1947 – STEPHEN SPIELBERG – Film director

19
1790 – SIR WILLIAM EDWARD PARRY – English sailor and arctic explorer

20
1868 – HARVEY FIRESTONE – American innovator of the tyre

21
1959 – FLORENCE GRIFFITH-JOYNER – American track athlete

DECEMBER

22
1858 – GIACOMO PUCCINI – Italian opera composer

23
1933 – EMPEROR AKIHITO – Japanese emperor

24
1932 – SIR COLIN COWDREY – Former England cricket captain

25
1642 – SIR ISAAC NEWTON – English scientist, discoverer of gravitation

26
1893 – MAO TSE-TUNG – Chinese statesmen

27
1822 – LOUIS PASTEUR – French scientist

28
1954 – DENZEL WASHINGTON – American actor

DECEMBER

29
1972 – JUDE LAW – British actor

30
1865 – RUDYARD KIPLING – English writer

31
1869 – HENRI MATISSE – French artist

NOTES

NOTES

NOTES

NOTES

NOTES

NOTES

NOTES

NOTES

NOTES